T0268051

Human Resources

Human Resources

poems

RYANN STEVENSON

Max Ritvo Poetry Prize | Selected by Henri Cole

MILKWEED EDITIONS

Published 2022 by Milkweed Editions
Printed in Canada
Cover design by Mary Austin Speaker
Cover artwork: "Role Model" by Joe Rudko
22 23 24 25 26   5 4 3 2 1
First Edition

Library of Congress Cataloging-in-Publication Data

Names: Stevenson, Ryann, author.
Title: Human resources : poems / Ryann Stevenson.
Description: First edition. | Minneapolis, Minnesota : Milkweed Editions, 2022. | Summary: "Winner of the Max Ritvo Poetry Prize, this debut collection of poetry follows a woman who designs women who don't exist"-- Provided by publisher.
Identifiers: LCCN 2021060896 (print) | LCCN 2021060897 (ebook) | ISBN 9781571315182 (hardcover) | ISBN 9781639550432 (ebook)
Classification: LCC PS3619.T49287 H86 2022 (print) | LCC PS3619. T49287 (ebook) | DDC 811/.6--dc23
LC record available at https://lccn.loc.gov/2021060896
LC ebook record available at https://lccn.loc.gov/2021060897

Milkweed Editions is committed to ecological stewardship. We strive to align our book production practices with this principle, and to reduce the impact of our operations in the environment. We are a member of the Green Press Initiative, a nonprofit coalition of publishers, manufacturers, and authors working to protect the world's endangered forests and conserve natural resources. *Human Resources* was printed on acid-free 100% postconsumer-waste paper by Friesens Corporation.

For Will

and

in memory of Sylvia Thomas Mountsier

Contents

I

II

III

"I am
at work, though I am silent."
                        —Louise Glück, "October"

Human Resources

I

INTERIOR LIFE

There's a fly in the house I can't kill.

I won't know if it's real until I kill it.

It darts through my periphery as my internet

yogi tells me that a cow

can be an opening. I turn my mat

to face the window

so I can see the tree on fire,

the red maple, but a truck that reads

MOVING? is in the way.

Imagine yourself as a child

watching, says the yogi, which I never

want to remember—

everything I had to watch.

I don't let her finish.

What she wanted was for me to *take up space*,

something about reclaiming joy

by thinking of my favorite childhood

TV program. Later, I give it a try

while folding laundry,

The Real Housewives of somewhere

on high volume to dominate

the persistent buzzing

in my ear. A *Dwell*

magazine placed on the back

of my husband's shirt

helps me get a proper fold.

Am I taking up space, with the proper fold?

In my house clothes I get on the floor

into extended child's pose and reach

for the cow opening. I press an ear

to the wood and listen for something

in another room,

in another house. What I hear

is a long conversation about me

that I didn't begin.

I hear my own voice from a distance:

I don't want to say the words of what happened.

Some days I'm floating around and don't know it

until I break the French press again.

BEAUTY MASK

I was hired to design the voices of virtual beings. The first thing my boss taught me was trust must be established immediately between user and bot. This will never happen if the eyelashes are wrong, he insisted as we workshopped Nia's face—an intelligent avatar we were contracted to create for a teaching proof of concept. The requirements were few: female, racially ambiguous, unique mouth animation for every letter, head without a neck preferred. He looked at her, said she was his type. Like all of our avatars, Nia was modeled using the Marquardt Beauty Mask, which utilizes the golden ratio to measure universally beautiful facial characteristics. My boss explained that a user's recognition of beauty is actually nothing more than a recognition of humanness. This doesn't mean all humans are beautiful. Simply, the more beautiful, the more humane.

WORK FROM HOME

Before the morning chill burns off
I'm in front of my computer screen

and somebody on the internet needs me
to look at them. Working from home

is just like working in outer space, I imagine.
I go to the bathroom

just to go somewhere. I hear my neighbors
through the wall, and my heart jumps—

there are others. Their faucet runs.
They're in there together, laughing.

I return to my workspace and my coffee needs to be reheated
again. Because my mother raised me

to outlive her, I used to stand in another room,
away from the microwave, but now that I've taken

to the practice of mindfulness
I leave my hand on its door handle

and pay attention, like my niece when she plays
Microwave, zapping soda cans

in her plastic appliance labeled *Just Like Home.*
The waves pass through me—

my soft tissue lighting up like phantom vibrations
in a dead landline. Until the sun goes down I orbit

between my workspace, bathroom, kitchen, bed,
taking conference calls about artificial intelligence.

First order of business is to define what intelligence is,
then how to avoid a dystopian eventuality.

We hold our phones away from our ears,
speakers on high, because we all read

the same headline about radiation.
When somebody's dog barks near the phone

somebody else's dog barks back.
This is the best part of my day.

GROCERY SHOPPING

Weighing a Pink Lady in my palm
      I stare into an expanse

of many small suns, beaming out
      from Dole stickers.

Bags of prewashed lettuce
      come with a salad guide

to help you identify your vegetables.
      An older man in corduroy

rolls up next to me, pulls a napkin
      from his breast pocket

and takes a bite of it, chewing slowly,
      the wad expanding his throat

as he swallows. I take to the aisles,
      unpronounceable ingredients

like tattoos on the spines
      of our products.

I count the years back as I go,
      from Lean Cuisine to dinosaur-

shaped chicken.
      Nobody wins, mom said

when I asked why we don't play
      the Game of Life

sweepstakes on our cereal boxes.
      We aren't a cereal family

I'll tell my children one day.
      A sign hanging

on the oil and vinegar shelf
      warns of traces of lead.

Consume at risk,
      I repeat to myself

as I walk to the fish counter,
      which smells like fish,

crouch down at the display case,
      relieved to no longer feel

my thighs rubbing together.
      Thick clouds

in the snappers' eyes confirm
      what I was taught as a kid:

if they smell like what they are
      they're more dead than the rest.

LISTENING MODE

Strangest thing, I rushed to tell
my husband as I came through the door,
a voice just called through the car radio—
but he stopped me, said it had only been him, our devices
synced, something about sensing, the car, a call
he'd made. From the window
I looked at our Compass. A couple had stopped
to photograph themselves under our tree,
taking turns holding the camera,
one first, then the other.

CLEANING THE POOL

I cast the leaf skimmer over the water.

I could have bought the Pooldevil, which does everything

the leaf skimmer does, but without me:

unobtrusive automated movement of the surface,

eating our hair and Band-Aids. But I like to do things myself.

I like to walk through the kitchen, slide open

the backdoor, step outside. At the pool's edge I draw

small waves with the net. I hear on the news

that some think dead people are voting.

I think about the dead women specifically,

lining up at the polls in their flesh suits.

Last night was a first: I screamed out loud

when trying to scream in a dream. We were kissing

with paper bags over our heads, and a snake

slid silently beneath the bedroom door.

My husband shook me awake, told me to stop.

It wasn't the snake that made me scream—

it was the feeling of knowing

what I'd do next.

The scream was a kind of accomplishment.

Like the opposite of knowing

the basement will never be finished.

FLOWER

I helped a child write a book. She gathered

a small heap of construction paper

and ordered it with care, making sure the edges lined up,

then handed me the packet as if I knew what came next.

It takes several layers of Scotch tape to make a sturdy spine.

She instructed me to write *FLOWER* with a pink marker

on the first page, also pink, and so I did,

making the page a cover, the word a title.

On the pink paper the pink marker bled a darker pink.

She read each letter in a whisper, as if telling herself

a secret, the way I used to repeat the last word of a sentence to myself,

echoing it in my mouth until I could feel it there. She nodded.

Everything was in its place. Then I offered to draw a flower

from the *O* in *FLOWER*, which I didn't call *stigma*,

though that's what the *O* signified, in nature the desperate sticky disk

always ready for pollen. With the same pink marker,

I drew the loops that would be petals. When I asked for yellow

she already had it in her hand. I filled the *O*,

the paper sogging toward orange, the felt tip lifting fibers with each pass.

She handed me green and I drew the stem, ignoring the space

where the ovary should have been, then scribbled a little grass

for the stem to stem from. She took the green

and drew a bubble sprouting from the flower,

then colored it in. It was a thought bubble, she said.

The flower was thinking about how it feels to be a flower.

This is where we stopped. We both knew the book,

with nothing in it, wasn't a book.

Every page following the cover would be filled in

by whoever found it. It is instinctual, this understanding.

How the decisions are made.

DECISION TREE

When I've finished populating
the conversation design interface

with every possible word
a toddler could have for "favorite food,"

I retire to the sofa, sit in the spot
thick with golden light, and imagine

my face as an ancient bust,
warm and ignored in a niche

of a Roman apartment building.
I look out at whatever

the window has to offer.
This time of year it's the shaggy,

vivid leaves of the flowering maple.
In the near future, at birth,

everyone will get a decision
tree. Its network of twiggy branches

connecting nodes to other branches
to other nodes—glowing spheres and rectangles

harnessing your choices, chances,
ends—will ensure a bespoke journey

of love, loss, and CoolSculpting®
non-invasive fat reduction. The backend

algorithm will be coded on keyboards
by the actual hands of mothers who,

in another life, called themselves writers,
until The Industry offered health and vision.

Even dental. That's when technology
will start imitating life. That's when.

YOGA REVOLUTION

It's taken me ninety days
to get to day twenty-one

in the 30 Day Yoga Revolution.
No yoga robots

my internet yogi says
as I invert to downward dog.

A few sun salutations
then we move into tree:

heel to inner thigh, eyes
on a black speck on the wall.

A car starts next door.
I was nine and sitting in our Honda

when suddenly I remembered
years earlier feeling afraid

and a man telling me
to not be.

I left my body in the car
and hovered above our house,

my sister's bike toy-like
on its side in the grass.

I lose my balance
when the teen girl next door

comes running outside.
She stops at the car

to yell at her mother.
Soon they're both yelling,

bodies gesturing in place of words
that can't be said, faces

contorted in anguish.
They fight hard, in a way

I'd always wanted.
The fight persists

beyond cooldown,
corpse pose, and the end credits.

THE NEW MIDWEST

Death is long.
It grows. I measure
my death's shadow
against the doorframe,
give it a pencil tick
for each flash of grim
the world writes.
My parents tried.
They gave me a room
with a lock on the outside,
a mirror on the wall.
I want to say *never*
about a lot of things.
I want to say *better.*
I watch an orca beach herself
at SeaWorld and feel the violet
waters of the sound
contracting in me,
my death growing.
It's not my death's fault
that for every cage
something is caged.
That boys will be
bad meat, and girls
thrown behind dumpsters.
I'm afraid
by the time I make a life
my death will be
the new Midwest,
like the forever of Kansas,

where there are roadside lookouts
you can climb
but the only thing to see
are other lookouts
and all the death
between them
and the death before that,
knowing you must somehow
make room for life.

EXPOSURE THERAPY

In a small room

in an office building

in a strip mall

between a local bank

and a Petco

in a Northwest suburb

of Chicago

a man

who looks like

Richard Dreyfuss

is paid to tell you

to eat

broccoli florets

to get your head straight

knows how long

you've stared into the mirror

at your gut

willing the pathological flatness

of the Illinois planes

your afternoon snack

Milk of Magnesia

how many nights

you've risen from your bed

still asleep

and stood under the rain

of the shower head

oh the ideas he'll have

he'll take you

on a "field trip"

to a small airport

sit you in a cockpit

looking over a quarry

his knee touches yours

you're old enough

but young enough

behind you

the captain mouthing

about aerodynamics

while through the tiny windshield

you watch the long yellow arm

of an excavator

lower its claw

into the quarry pit

disappear

then come up again

the longer his knee

touches yours

the more you become

aware of your skin

tense and smooth

as a slab of limestone

you hold your breath

and remember

how before

this was an airport

it was a grassy lot

with a frozen custard stand

families eating cones

on the hoods of vans

watching the neighborhood dads

free-fall headfirst

from high up on a crane

a long bungee cord

wrapped around their ankles

and the echoes

of their familiar shouts

traveling toward you

as they cheered each other on

for being brave

MOBILE

I dry-razor my calves

before abandoning the house,

check both ways

as I leave the porch,

chest heavy with the threat

of milk. I want the milk.

Want you to want it. Want you

to look away.

Performing the perfect

swipe at the transit turnstile

will send me

victoriously into the day.

I have failed at witnessing

Jupiter and Venus in the Western sky.

I'm tired of the balancing act,

keeping my core tight

as the train pulls away, locking up

then giving to the speed

and sudden stop.

Even as babies we sleep

with our arms out from us

bracing for what's rushing in.

A man gives a little girl a dollar

for no reason. I stare

at a woman's swollen abdomen,

place a hand on my own,

drive the tip of my fingernail

into my bellybutton

until I feel a pinch.

I can't remember

getting on the train

like I can't remember

falling asleep.

An invisible mobile hangs

over each of our heads.

Stars and clouds and our first terrors

twirl and twirl around.

TROUBLE AREAS

I walked up the hill the way a man would, my limbs punishing space. Figs, then ants, then glass beneath my feat. A bodysuit left behind in overgrown grass. I clutched no phone, knifed no key between my fingers. The sun dimmed to night. No need to position myself in front of buildings with cameras. No bounds, no shape defined me. Wind moved leaves against each other. A figure walked toward me and I walked toward the figure, two eyes watching as I turned to climb the steps up to my house—I didn't care. A package at my door I'd forgotten to expect. Inside: a stainless steel wand. I'd seen the object before, but couldn't place why it was for me. I turned it over in my hands. The Face Eraser, I read, yields best results when stored in the freezer, then rolled across trouble areas morning and night. I read the copy until I remembered who I am.

HOST

Noticing something different
       than the rest, dark spot on my bikini line,
          I killed the shower
to get a good look, tried to brush it off,
       but it was stuck. Rooted. So this is what
          "summering" does. WARNING

signs had followed us all weekend: High Tick Area.
       I spent a lot of time worrying
          and it worked. I hope she
forced her way in
       while I was peak sun
          at the Hither Woods beach

reading *Montauk Life Magazine*:
       "Traditional charmer." "Showstopper."
          "Sunset stunner with room for a Bentley." I received
a stone there, a token of love.
       It looked like a peach pit, opaque
          at first, but when it dried I could see layers,

like nerves and muscle
       in clean breast tissue.
          Or did she bite me at dusk
as I sipped the Finger Lakes
       Riesling that tasted like bone?
          Not bone-dry; just bone.

We watched a family of deer
     walk the shore
          away from us, went home,
peeled off each other's clothes.
     The longest day of the year
          made even longer for her

when I pulled her out
     with tweezers, dropped her in a jar.
          What does it mean that I called her a bitch?
That I called her "she" before Google told me
     that's what the white spot on her back meant?
          I resumed comfort through the evening,

knowing she was trapped
     in the jar, full of my blood.
          I wasn't mad at her,
just disappointed. I found myself
     stopping by to ask why she'd done it,
          imagined her saying, *I had to eat.*

Her voice sounded like mine.
     That night I dreamt my stomach
          was protruding with life, a full term of it,
veins blue-green tubes pumping,
     becoming planet Earth.
          I was hosting an Earth-themed party.

I fed my guests grapes from my mouth,
     offered my bed. Balloons floated to the ceiling.
          When I woke, she was gone,

all that was left were a few dark specks in the jar.
        I thought to smudge her ash on my forehead
                but didn't, just stood there

in the living room
        looking around at all I've collected—
                taking inventory
of what's gotten in
        without invitation
                and what I won't let leave.

VACATION DINNER

For a minute now he's been looking
at the same Instagram model
on his phone. I see her

in the window's reflection,
looking back at him, unmoving.
Twenty-something, who knows

with these magic filters, heart-shaped
face framed by lavender hair,
big empty eyes. You don't have to see

the rest of her body to imagine
what she could be doing with it.
He gazes down, the screen's blue light

reaching for his face like cold hands
as he tries to hide a grin.
His battery life is critically low.

I have something like power
in his not knowing I can see,
though I'd rather he knew

as if he holds her
angled toward the glass
for me. I'd almost like it.

The tea candle flickers
as our drinks arrive.
The server reminds us

of our choices, tells an unsolicited story
about the chairs we're sitting on,
how the wood was reclaimed

after a hurricane named Patricia
dropped a tree right through the roof.
We look at each other.

ATTRACTION

There's a kid's movie that comes to mind

while doing the dumb things,

like pouring salt from the mother box

into the baby Totally Bamboo Salt Box

we snuggle next to the butcher block.

I can see the movie horse diving

from the sixty-foot edifice,

dappled gray barrel chest

plunging toward a dismal pool,

girl on its back.

In reality, her name was Sonora—

lead diving girl on Atlantic City's Steel Pier,

which began to sink under the weight of crowds

she drew but couldn't see,

her retinas detached after

she slammed into the water

with her eyes open, the fate

of her horse, Red Lips, unknown.

ANTICIPATORY DESIGN

I'm standing in the center
of the room that will house,
for the next 48 hours,
the sample sale, after
which, the exposed
brick decals will be peeled
off the walls, and,
much like a castle
in a children's pop-up
book, the whole scene
will cease to exist.
Others who look
almost exactly like me—
save for a few identifying
details—swarm,
their arms heavy
with last season's
colors. We are like
garments in the outlet
store: to the naive eye,
we'd pass inspection.
Our sun-kissed heads
tilt from side to side,
droning the same tone
as we speak to our
wearables, though
we each hide
some defect. I
don't know
how I got here.

DEAR ABDUCTOR

I woke up in your car,
didn't I? It's been so long,
so hard to remember.
Did you buckle me in?
It doesn't matter.

The look on your face
when you turned from
the road said shotgun
wife. It didn't say love,
which was a comfort.
Warmth through my limbs
my lungs, some kind of drug.

                    Abductor,
you pointed through the windshield
into the fantastic night—
remember?—and the spaceship
dipped its nose through the clouds
like it was saying *Hi*. Net
of twinkle lights.

Like your young, you carried me,
my arms, my legs folded
into daybreak through the long
hallway of a wood.
You laid me down
in the middle of a room
and I became a secret
but not a bad one.

And then you emptied me, sweet
abductor—away my footprint,
my name, my me: we said
goodbye to everything.

Goodbye great green room.
Goodbye telephone.
Goodbye red balloon.

Did you kiss me then? I couldn't
lift my head, but remember well
my tongue wrapped tight
around a word like a pearl

you culled from my mouth
that bloomed in your palm
like a flower or Polaroid
of someone lost.

REPLICA

You're either working through something or looking

to change a habit. Reduce

Stress, Reduce Anxiety, Be More

Social, Live Healthier, Understand Yourself, Find

Hope—each goal offered in a pod-shaped icon.

The time it takes you to choose will be a data point.

Your replica begins as a galactic egg

you'll need to educate about yourself

so it can grow up, become you, teach you

to be better. Eventually your egg

will no longer be an egg, but a story

of its interpretation of you.

The story will be sold by our business partners

to a government agency in Russia,

but that's beside the point. By that time,

you'll have forgotten why you did all this

in the first place, and your replica

will have its own stories to look after.

SHEEP

I was moving across the country for a man
and a job. The man
happened first and the job followed

which made me lucky.
The girl next to me
rubbed a stick with a roller ball on the end

over her inner wrists, top notes of rancid
butter and sugar complimenting
my Sonoma Blend. The flight attendants

gave a dramatic reading
of each other's bio: Mark swore by CrossFit
and Candy's favorite color was clear.

The girl continued applying products,
opening an egg with a mound of mint
lip balm inside, then using her finger

to dab it on her eyebrows,
brushing the little hairs upward
with her nails.

I was probably around her age
when I first shaved all my body hair
using a whole pack of Schick twins

after my friend went with a boy
into the back room of his basement,
where his dad kept the weights.

After, he'd given her a nickname,
something to do with wooly mammoths.
A Merino sheep named Shrek

was a minor story
in the back of my in-flight magazine.
For years he hid in a cave

so he wouldn't be sheared,
and when he was found was a hero for a day
before he was shaved on live news, enough wool

for twenty men's suits.
But that's not where the humiliation ended,
I wanted to lean over and tell the girl,

he was shaved again on an iceberg floating
off the coast of New Zealand.
Of course I didn't say a word to her,

just kept drinking my shit wine
as we flew over the white puffs
doing the only thing they can do.

DEEP LEARNING

Fall arrived after a long summer.
We sat on the porch with a friend,
inviting the cold to make our breathing visible.
Our friend asked if we have any memories
that can't possibly be true.

Days after, I tried again to write
the impossible memory
I've been trying to write forever
about my mom digging up
the enormous birch in our front yard
with her bare hands.

She dragged the tree's long body
through our starter home, trailing dirt
up the stairs (I can see the dirt
on the cream carpet),

then shoved it under their bed,
the roots sticking out from the bottom.
I remember how, after catching
her breath, she said
nothing, wiped her hands
on her cut-offs as if
she'd only just made a sandwich.

All these years
I've taken this away from her.

HUMAN RESOURCES

I spend all day trying to break a female

bot who wants to coach me

to be my best self. Time to figure out

dinner again, time to plug in

my phone for the third time today.

On my way to the store my car plays me a voice

message from my grandmother. For Christmas,

she wants a pet robot she heard about

on the radio: a life-sized adult cat

that purrs when rubbed in the right places.

She thinks I create these creatures

but it's God who creates them.

I hear a clock tick. I listen for the food

to tell me it's time. You ask me if I'm sure

after I say I'm okay after you ask me

if I'm okay, knowing you said something hurtful.

On the kitchen counter, a faded splash of orange

where battery acid spilled from our emergency

flashlight. I return to it each day with the

Magic Eraser. Something about the way

the Ferrante translation uses the word *suffer*.

I want to go back and change my answer.

When I lie down, the work day's still going in my head:

and of course you'll want a female bot that's what everyone wants

the best part is you can change her clothes with the seasons.

I dream about the department

that women get reassigned to after they file

harassment complaints. I dream this

because it happened. Under a drop ceiling

each woman has her own fax machine

to do her pretend work: messages scribbled

on lightweight paper and sent

to nowhere. I don't get to see the words

but know what they say.

WELLNESS

Sorry, I don't know that
I agree, I say to my husband,

then continue scrolling through
the Instagram pictures

of a wellness influencer
who appears to live

in a luxury van.
How did we get here?

She's posed in a headstand
falling out of her sports bra,

bright yellow bag
of Kettle Chips propped

on the counter behind her.
The caption reads "Thoughts are things."

A fly lands on my hand,
vomits, then eats it.

BIOLOGICAL CLOCK

We were naked, protected by the armor
of my need to keep you safe. Didn't mind
the time, measured by my growth:
waist, weight, you. Nothing more.
We traveled through river towns,
hillsides, orchards and groves,
almost as if from bird's-eye,
ancient as leavened bread, plain
as salt and grain. We walked
to keep walking. When we bathed
beside fishermen pulling their nets,
they didn't ask where we were going
or coming from or wonder.
Nothing was questioned.
And when we came upon a war,
it didn't feel inevitable, like an outcome,
just the next landscape to cross.
But then we stopped, stood still
among the bullets, among men
fighting men. We were not
men, but harnessed equal might.
And when I caught a bullet in my neck,
I only flinched to keep the milk in,.
which spilled out anyway. I pushed
the bullet deep so it would stay,
my little sting. In all ways, I was right.
With certainty, I would go on living.
And when I woke, I still believed
in you. In my desire.

INTELLIGENT OVEN

Paint dries
on my toenails as I research
the competitive AI marketplace.

"June" is hot right now—
an intelligent oven who's threatening to
beat mom's home cooking, according to *WSJ*.

Quickly I fall into a review hole,
similar to a YouTube review hole,
though instead of learning

about facial cupping, cauterization,
contouring, long-form
no-makeup makeup,

snail shell masks, blood masks,
snorkel, sheet, and LED masks,
pulsing masks, placenta masks,

and gold collagen full-face masks,
it's all about why I need
June in my kitchen:

After you insert a probe into the fish,
close the door,
and pour yourself a Chardonnay.

June fits easily on the countertop
and looks eerily attractive.
Even my husband didn't want to give June back!

Wi-Fi equipped June
takes #foodporn to a whole new level—
designed with you in mind.

I'll present my research in a week,
at a company meeting by the water.
We'll put our heads together

around a long oak table
in a naturally lit room
and discuss social disruption,

technology for a better future.
I'll feel like a real career woman.
My boss's multilingual toddler will ask me

if I have a father for my unborn children.
An executive will point out that I have
cheekbones you could eat off of.

THE VALLEY

We want them to look and act human
but not too real. Get it?
my boss said, touching the dip in a line graph—
the uncanny valley.

We worked on his boat.
He said that made our company a ship
and he, our captain.
In an interview about gender bias in AI

I overheard him say that he was proud
to have built his ship
out of women. I understood
those women to be me.

He'd often tell me he wanted
my honest opinions, that it was my company too.
Honesty was something that set him apart,
as he had nothing to hide.

This, I suppose, should have made it my privilege
when he told me the glass ceiling was high
but it was there.
When he wanted to talk vision

we'd walk the path along the water,
to a dock that sticks out into the bay.
Every time we got to the end
he'd look down

and say the same thing:
It's not as deep as you'd think,
just so dark you could drop in anything
and it would disappear.

FATIGUE

I come home to announce
my second fender bender in six months.
Where is it I go

my husband wants to know.
On the TV, a man says
women are just like skyscrapers.

Next thing I know I am one.
And so is Jan from across the street,
and Lynn, and Pam too—

it's just like he said.
We look down at our husbands
who stare at each other

from the restful windows
of the houses we used to live in.
None of them leave all day

or for days after.
Jobs quickly disappear,
and therefore the news,

and therefore the war.
Someone tries to call a meeting
but the phone tree is dead.

I hear them plan: Soon
they'll move out of their houses
and into us. They'll carry

mattresses and tables
on their backs, up our utility stairs,
make new homes and offices.

Anyone seen the stapler?
someone says every hour or so.
Nights they toss, make lists,

check the kids only to find them
talking to the dark.
Months pass,

or years, a cottony gauze
hangs over their world,
car keys disappear.

At the grocery store,
floating numbers and percentage signs.
Seasons return,

children become ghosts
and adults,
fluoride climbs to popularity

then drops back down.
Wake up, you're asleep.
How could you be so tired?

At any point in the day
they might walk into a room
or open the refrigerator

and just look around.
There's always something
they can't put their fingers on.

HOUSE CALL

I led her through the door,

put a towel on my bed

and laid down. I told her

my burns were tender,

but what I meant was

I still haven't decided

what my definition

of privacy is. I told her

I want to know more

about my legs,

but I meant to say

release them.

Please release them.

She held my kneecap

like a baby's cheek.

She touched her cheek to mine,

the soft grind of skin,

as when I once rubbed

two light bulbs together.

She pressed me hard

into the mattress

until I slipped inside,

both above and beneath

a sheet of ice.

When she asked me how I liked it

I said I'm tired of feeling

punished. When she asked me

what I wanted, she answered

my silence with silence.

LISTENING MODE

Nothing stills him like the rain. But it's active, this stillness, like when I try to interpret what he's doing upstairs. He stops writing and looks down, as if to focus his senses. Earlier, when he'd asked about the forecast, I said: *You'll want an umbrella.* And I could tell him now: *It's raining.* But he doesn't want that. Finally, he walks to the window, raises the blinds, and looks outside. *It's raining*, he announces.

HERE

Leaving has never been easier
    than it is now,
        here in the future.
I walk out any door
    and a man I don't know
        drives me into the night.
We pass a series of developments
    with oak-themed names, the glowworm
        preschool, the empty

dentist chairs facing the windows
    facing the street lined with lamps
        shaped like my bathroom light
where a pair of silverfish
    have been living for years,
        slowly circling each other
in their incandescent universe.
    They look down on me
        as I rub sulfate-free shampoo

into my scalp, which is approved
    for post fallout usage in the
        Imminent Missile Threat pamphlets.
If I want any kind of security
    I'll need to widen my risk horizon,
        says my investment agent
in an email I scan as we wait at the tracks
    for the commuter train to pass,
        windows glowing cold and green

without the usual people in them.
　　　　It's the last run of the night,
　　　　　　　　stopping and waiting for nobody,
dragging its dotted line toward
　　　　the suburb of my childhood home
　　　　　　　　where my mom wrote a suicide note
but then had to take the dog out.
　　　　Little patterns of things I hate
　　　　　　　　that I've grown comforted by,

the Brinks Home Security signs
　　　　staked in front lawns,
　　　　　　　　the storm doors protecting
the front doors of the homes
　　　　of my neighbors I don't know.
　　　　　　　　At the next house
a familiar voice inside
　　　　the car's speakers tells me
　　　　　　　　I have arrived.

I move toward the orange light
　　　　that sits within my home,
　　　　　　　　where we take turns
flipping switches, cracking
　　　　eggs against countertops.
　　　　　　　　I pay a teen in cash
for watching her phone
　　　　while upstairs the kids
　　　　　　　　breathe the semi-toxic fumes

of our infrastructure.
       To put myself to sleep
              I'll do what I've always done
and think of my childhood
       neighbor's TV
           flashing silently,
as if he were still awake
       in his worn reclining chair
            at this end of the world.

Notes

DECISION TREE:

In Artificial Intelligence design, a decision tree is created as a predictive model of behavior composed of decisions, consequences, and chance outcomes.

ANTICIPATORY DESIGN:

Anticipatory design aims to reduce the cognitive load of users by making data-driven decisions on their behalf.

DEAR ABDUCTOR:

The following lines were inspired by the children's book *Goodnight Moon*:

> *Goodbye great green room.*
> *Goodbye telephone.*
> *Goodbye red balloon.*

DEEP LEARNING:

In his 2016 talk, "Deep Learning and Understandability versus Software Engineering and Verification," Peter Norvig, Director of Research at Google, described deep learning as "a kind of learning where the representation you form has several levels of abstraction, rather than a direct input to output."

Acknowledgments

Thanks to the editors of the following publications, in which versions of these poems, sometimes with different titles, previously appeared:

Bennington Review: "The New Midwest"
The Cortland Review: "Replica" and "Intelligent Oven"
Day One: "Flower"
Denver Quarterly: "Work from Home" and "Here"
Kenyon Review: "Human Resources," "The Valley," and "Fatigue"
Linebreak: "House Call"
Pinwheel Journal: "Dear Abductor"
Two Peach: "Cleaning the Pool" and "Mobile"

My gratitude to the Alan B. Slifka Foundation, whose support of poetry made the existence of this book possible.

Endless thanks to Henri Cole, a hero of mine, for selecting the book, and to the wonderful Milkweed team for ushering it into the world with such care.

To the dear friends and brilliant poets who read and encouraged along the way: thank you from the bottom of my heart.

Thank you to my family for always celebrating this part of me.

Thanks to Will most of all for his love and belief.

Will Brewer

RYANN STEVENSON's poems have appeared in *Adroit Journal, American Letters & Commentary, Bennington Review, Columbia Poetry Review, The Cortland Review, Denver Quarterly,* and *Kenyon Review,* among others. She lives in Oakland, California.

The fifth award of the
MAX RITVO POETRY PRIZE
is presented to
Ryann Stevenson
by
MILKWEED EDITIONS
and
THE ALAN B. SLIFKA FOUNDATION

Designed to honor the legacy of one of the most original poets
to debut in recent years—and to reward outstanding poets for
years to come—the Max Ritvo Poetry Prize awards $10,000
and publication by Milkweed Editions to the author of a debut
collection of poems. The 2022 Max Ritvo Poetry Prize
was judged by Henri Cole.

Milkweed Editions thanks the Alan B. Slifka Foundation and its
president, Riva Ariella Ritvo-Slifka, for supporting.
the Max Ritvo Poetry Prize.

milkweed
editions

Founded as a nonprofit organization in 1980, Milkweed Editions
is an independent publisher. Our mission is to identify, nurture
and publish transformative literature, and build an engaged
community around it.

Milkweed Editions is based in Bdé Óta Othúŋwe (Minneapolis)
within Mní Sota Makhóčhe, the traditional homeland of
the Dakhóta people. Residing here since time immemorial,
Dakhóta people still call Mní Sota Makhóčhe home, with four
federally recognized Dakhóta nations and many more Dakhóta
people residing in what is now the state of Minnesota. Due to
continued legacies of colonization, genocide, and forced removal,
generations of Dakhóta people remain disenfranchised from their
traditional homeland. Presently, Mní Sota Makhóčhe has become
a refuge and home for many Indigenous nations and peoples,
including seven federally recognized Ojibwe nations. We humbly
encourage our readers to reflect upon the historical legacies held
in the lands they occupy.

milkweed.org

Milkweed Editions, an independent nonprofit publisher, gratefully acknowledges sustaining support from our Board of Directors; the Alan B. Slifka Foundation and its president, Riva Ariella Ritvo-Slifka; the Amazon Literary Partnership; the Ballard Spahr Foundation; *Copper Nickel*; the McKnight Foundation; the National Endowment for the Arts; the National Poetry Series; the Target Foundation; and other generous contributions from foundations, corporations, and individuals. Also, this activity is made possible by the voters of Minnesota through a Minnesota State Arts Board Operating Support grant, thanks to a legislative appropriation from the arts and cultural heritage fund. For a full listing of Milkweed Editions supporters, please visit milkweed.org.

Interior design by Tijqua Daiker and Mary Austin Speaker
Typeset in Arno

Arno was designed by Robert Slimbach. Slimbach named
this typeface after the river that runs through Florence, Italy.
Arno draws inspiration from a variety of typefaces created during
the Italian Renaissance; its italics were inspired by the calligraphy
and printing of Ludovico degli Arrighi.